The Waterman/Harewood Piano Series

Piano Playtime Studies

Very first studies
collected and edited by

Fanny Waterman

and

Marion Harewood

Faber Music Limited
London

The studies in this collection are really short pieces, each focused on one or more specific technical points. They will help develop equality of fingers, legato and staccato playing, singing tone and dynamics. At the same time the descriptive titles and illustrations will stimulate the player's imagination so that there will be no dividing line between technique and musical expression.

F.W. & M.H.

This collection © 1986 by Faber Music Ltd
First published in 1986 by Faber Music Ltd
3 Queen Square London WC1N 3AU
Music engraved by Jack Thompson
Illustrations by Juliet Clarke
Cover designed by M & S Tucker
Printed in England by Halstan & Co Ltd

CONTENTS

1 Pop goes the weasel!
Traditional

2 Pussy cat
Traditional

3 Up and down the ladder

Johann Burgmüller

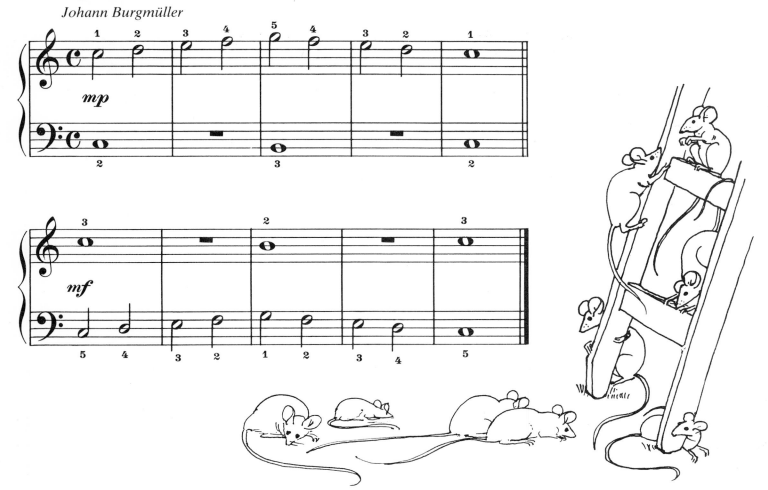

4 Gliding

Hermann Berens

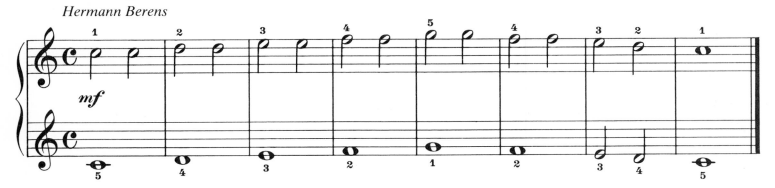

5 Skipping

Hermann Berens

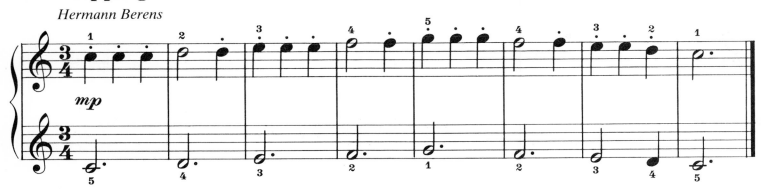

6   By the sea

Louis Köhler

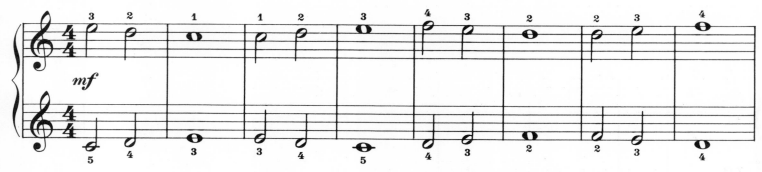

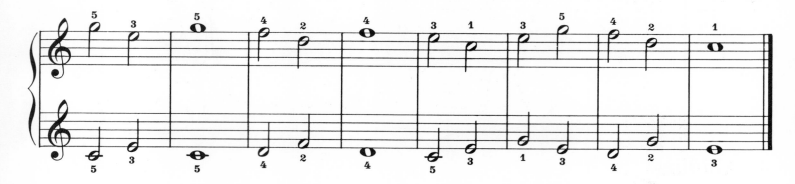

7   Giant footsteps

Louis Köhler

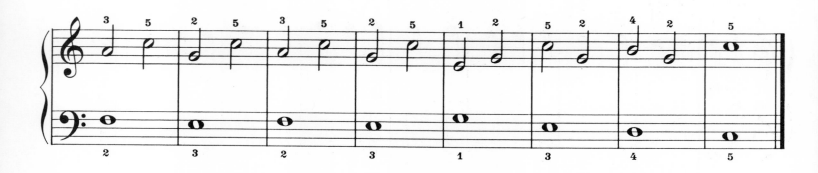

8 Singing together

Béla Bartók

Moderato

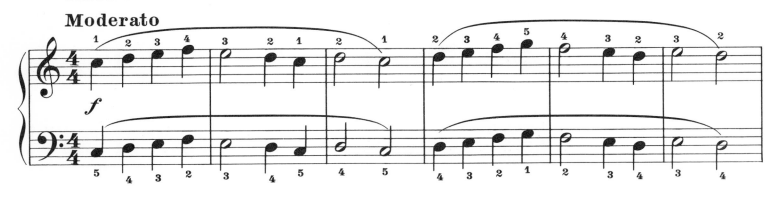

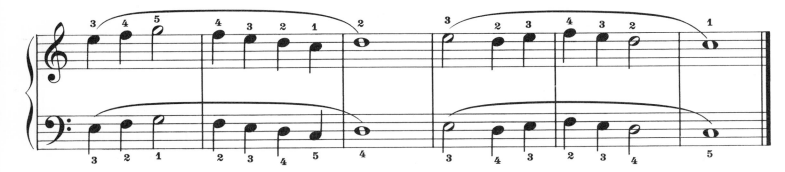

9 My shadow

Ferdinand Beyer

Andantino

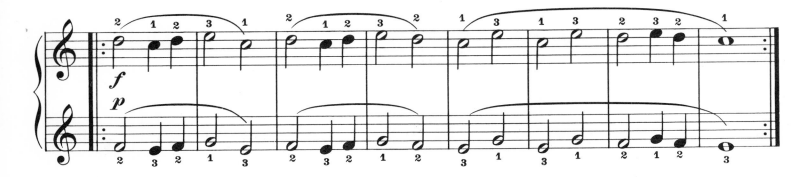

8

10 Bedtime story

Ferdinand Beyer

11 Bicycle ride

Cornelius Gurlitt

12 Little dancer

Daniel Türk

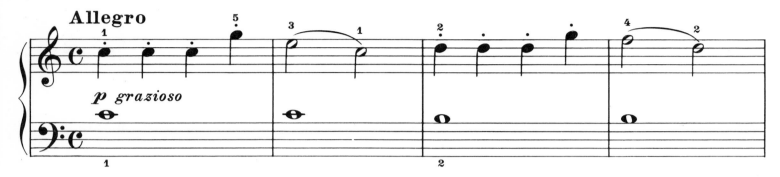

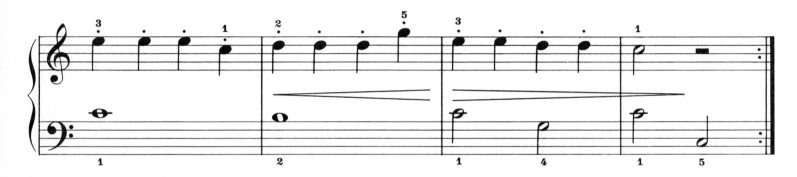

13 The robin

Daniel Türk

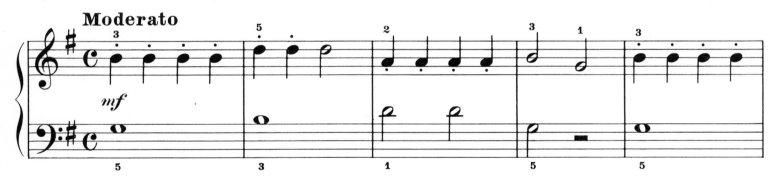

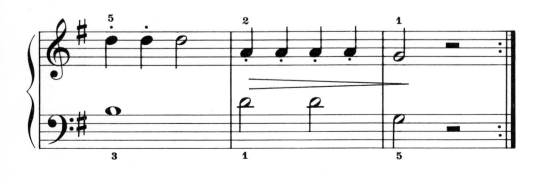

14 Hopping frog

Carl Czerny

15 Autumn

Carl Czerny

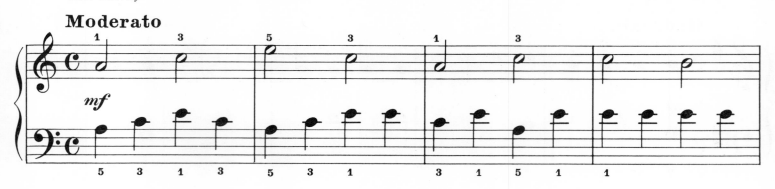

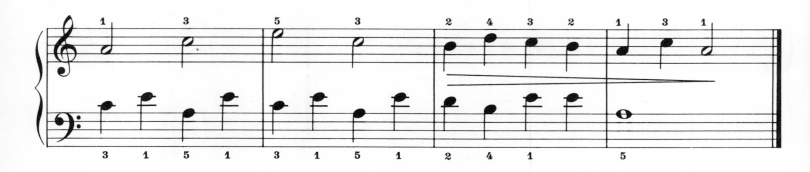

16 A walk in the country

Carl Czerny

Andantino

17 Rocking horse

Cornelius Gurlitt

Moderato

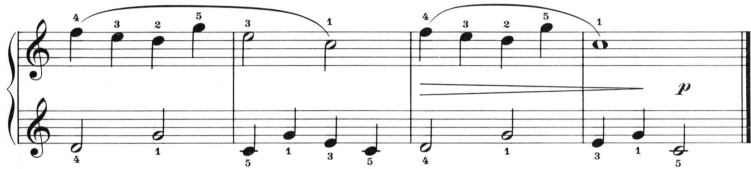

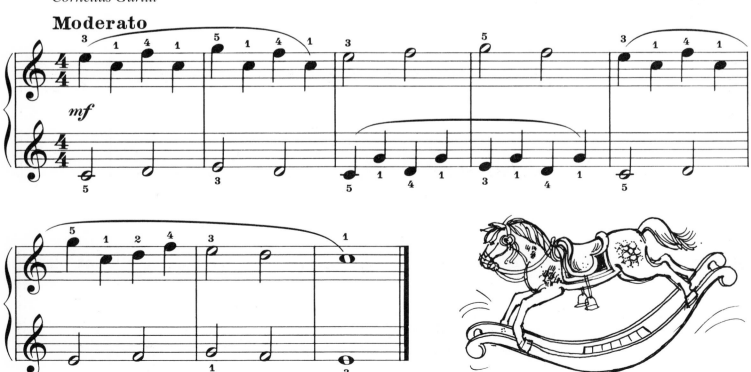

18 Pony trot

Ferdinand Beyer

Allegro

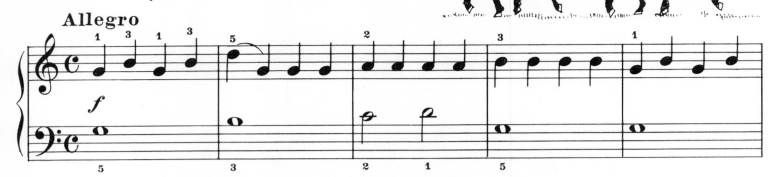

19 Soldiers on parade

Johann Burgmüller

Alla marcia

20 The haunted castle

Carl Czerny

Andante

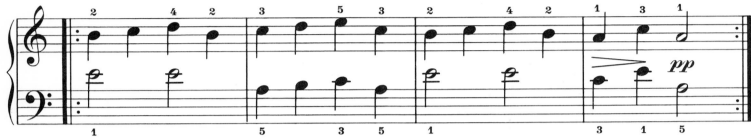

21 On your toes

E. Gnyesina

Grazioso

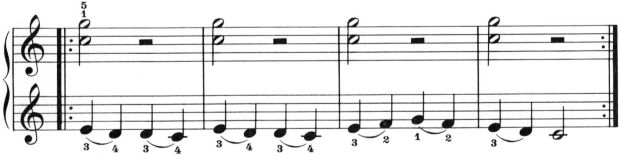

22 The church organ

F.W./M.H.

Largo

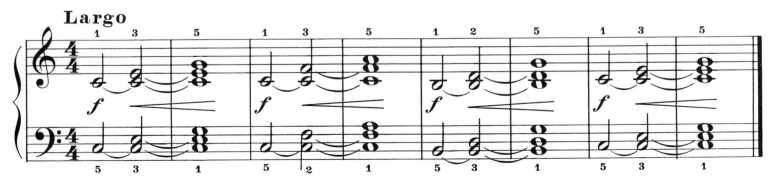

23 Fanfares

F.W./M.H.

24 Moon and stars

Ferdinand Beyer

25 Russian song

Dimitri Kabalevsky

Andante

26 Hungarian dance

Zoltán Kodály

Allegretto

27 Springtime

Daniel Türk

Allegretto

28 Elves and goblins

Carl Czerny

Allegretto